AF373004

To my beloved children,

With love and gratitude, this dedication celebrates our shared love of reading. May our literary adventures continue to inspire and deepen our connection, forever nourishing our souls.

A.C. LARC'S **LEARNING LIBRARY NUMBERS**

Text Copyright © 2023 by A.C. Larc
Layout Copyright © 2023 by A.C. Larc

First Printing, 2023

Illustration Credit: Olya F.

ISBN 979-8-9887292-2-8 (Hardcover)
ISBN 979-8-9887292-3-5 (Paperback)

To find out more visit
www.aclarcbooks.com

THIS BOOK
BELONGS TO

1 brilliant princess, wise and fair,

a leader with a heart that truly cares.

2 robots, gears spinning fast,

in a world of circuits, they have a blast.

3 playful monsters, wild and free,

skipping and laughing, as happy as can be.

4 magical fairies, making dreams come true,

spreading joy and laughter, in everything they do.

5 silly dragons, full of delight,

they fly and play from morning till night.

6 unicorns, they prance and play,

spreading magic and wonder throughout the day.

7 lovely mermaids, shimmering and bright,

in the depths of the ocean, a breathtaking sight.

8 trolls, kind and true,

spreading love and light in all they do.

9 ancient dinosaurs, stomping all around,

filling the land and air, with a loud thunderous sound.

10 ocean creatures, frolic in the deep blue sea,

with joy in their hearts, happy and free.

Help the fairy count the twinkling stars,

as they sprinkle their light from afar.

Help the troll count the mushrooms, one by one,

on the ground, they bask in the sun.

Help the mermaid count the seashells, shining bright,

treasures of the ocean, a wonderful delight.

Help the princess count the butterflies, flying by,

their wings painted with colors that catch the eye.

Count the baby dinosaurs, cute and small,

in ancient forests, they roam and crawl.

How many flowers are in unicorn glen?

A rainbow of blossoms, a magical blend.

My little reader, you're a counting machine,

from one to ten, you're the best I've seen.

Counting is a game, we love to play,

so have some fun, counting each and every day.